LEARN TO PLAY
ELECTRIC GUITAR

Nigel Hooper

Designed by Neil Francis

Additional designs by Joe Pedley

Studio photography by Howard Allman
Original music by Nigel Hooper

Edited by Caroline Hooper

Electric guitar consultant: David Kear
American consultant: Eric Allen
Photo research: Ruth King
Music setting: Eileen O'Brien
Series editor: Jane Chisholm
With thanks to Emma Danes

ALL ABOUT THE ELECTRIC GUITAR

This book will help you to get the most out of your electric guitar, whether or not you already know how to play. It contains music in lots of different styles, as well as hints about everything, from using effects to writing your own tunes and playing in a band. As you go through the book, you will learn new notes and musical words, with special techniques and signs explained simply and clearly. You can also find out about some famous electric guitarists.

Choosing an instrument

If you are choosing a second-hand guitar to buy, there are several things to look out for:

1. Check that the neck is in line with the body of the guitar. If it isn't, the guitar may go out of tune easily.

2. Make sure you can press the strings down comfortably all the way along the neck. If the action (the height of the strings above the fingerboard) is too high, the strings will be hard to press down. If the action is too low, the strings will buzz.

Machine head

Capstan

Nut

Sixth string

Headstock

Neck

Fret

First string

3. Check that the frets are parallel and not worn down. You can see whether the frets are parallel by holding the guitar up to eye level, horizontally, and looking along the length of the neck, toward the body.

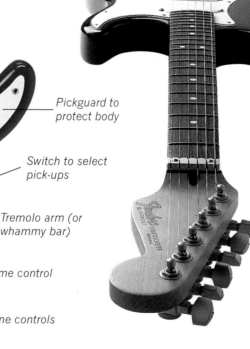

Pick-ups

Saddle

Pickguard to protect body

Switch to select pick-ups

Tremolo arm (or whammy bar)

Volume control

Tone controls

Bridge

Jack for electric lead

Strings

It is a good idea to change all your guitar strings at the same time. You can buy them in sets of six. Guitar strings come in different gauges (thicknesses). If you are a beginner, start with light- or medium-gauge strings. (The packet should say 0.008 or 0.009 for the first string.) You can find out how to change the strings on your guitar on page 17.

Using an amplifier

Electric guitars have to be amplified before you can hear them properly. A small amp (10 watt) is suitable for practicing, but it is always a good idea to use headphones to avoid disturbing other people. You can buy special headphones which plug directly into your guitar, or you can use an ordinary set of headphones which plug into your amplifier.

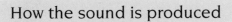

Headphones jack

Jack for guitar lead

How the sound is produced

When you play a string it vibrates. Small wire coils called pick-ups, on the body of an electric guitar, convert the string vibrations into electrical signals. These signals are sent to the amplifier and converted into sounds, which then come out of the loudspeaker.

Safety

Whenever you are using electrical equipment it is very important to take a few simple precautions.

Eric Clapton was born in England in 1945. He was heavily influenced by the American blues scene, especially by performers such as Chuck Berry, Muddy Waters and Big Bill Broonzy. During the sixties he developed his blues style in groups like the Yardbirds and Cream. Later he formed his own band, Derek and the Dominoes, producing the hit single *Layla*. Throughout the eighties and nineties Clapton pursued a career as a solo artist, with his album *From the Cradle*, released in 1994, still showing a huge influence from blues music. His distinctive style of playing has made him one of the world's most respected and accomplished guitarists.

Checklist for safety

- Keep leads and wires neat and out of the way. Never leave them lying around.

- Turn your equipment off and remove any plugs when you are not playing.

- Always keep drinks away from electrical equipment.

- If you have a problem with your guitar or amplifier, get help from the manufacturer or shop where you bought them. Never try to fix the problem yourself.

STARTING TO PLAY

How to hold your electric guitar

You can sit or stand to play the electric guitar. Whichever you choose to do, you must feel relaxed so that your fingers are free to move easily. If you sit, rest the body of the guitar on your right thigh, slanting towards you slightly so that you can see the strings. A stool or chair without arms is best. Electric guitars are fairly heavy, so if you stand up to play, you will need to use a strap. Adjust this so the guitar feels comfortable, keeping the neck a little higher than the main body of the guitar.

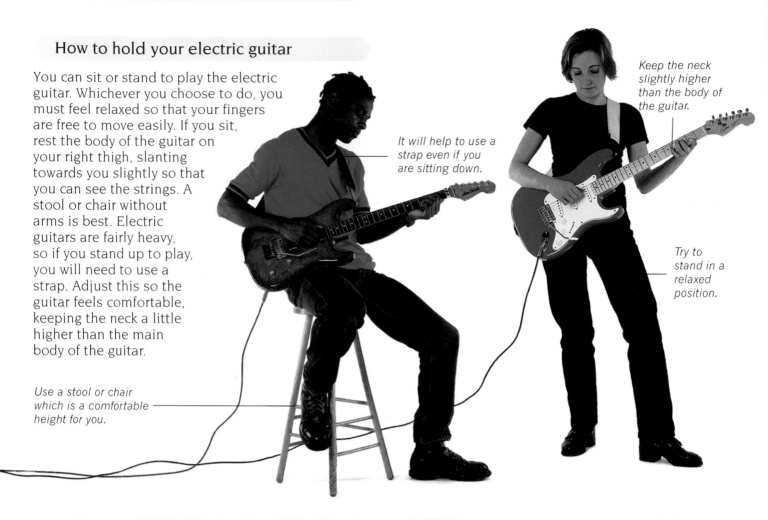

It will help to use a strap even if you are sitting down.

Keep the neck slightly higher than the body of the guitar.

Try to stand in a relaxed position.

Use a stool or chair which is a comfortable height for you.

Left-hand position

Rest your left thumb on the back of the guitar neck, between your first and second fingers, arching your hand so that only the tips of your fingers are near the strings. Practice pressing a string down just to the left of a fret. In the first few tunes, you use your first finger for the first fret, your second finger for the second fret, and so on.

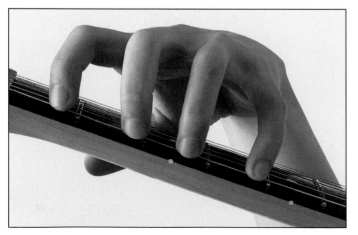

Right-hand position

For the first few tunes in the book, it is best to use a pick, sometimes called a plectrum. Hold the pick between your thumb and the side of your first finger, bending your finger slightly, but keeping your thumb straight. Rest the edge of your wrist lightly on the top end of the bridge. Play the strings by moving your wrist from side to side.

TUNING YOUR GUITAR

Always make sure each string is tuned to the correct note before you start to play. Turning the machine head counter-clockwise tightens the string and makes it sound higher. Turning it clockwise loosens the string, making it sound lower. You can tune your guitar in several different ways.

Relative tuning

One of the best ways to tune your guitar is by relative tuning. This means you tune one string (the sixth string) to the correct note, then use this to tune the other strings. First, make sure your sixth string is in tune. Then, tune each string in turn, following the instructions below. The numbered dots on this guitar neck show you which notes to use.

1. Play the note at the fifth fret of the sixth string and tune your fifth string so it exactly matches this note.

2. Play the note at the fifth fret of the fifth string and then tune your fourth string to this note.

3. Play the note at the fifth fret of the fourth string. Tune your third string to this note.

4. To tune the second string, play the note at the fourth (not fifth) fret of the third string.

5. Play the note at the fifth fret of the second string. Tune your first string to this note.

When you have finished, it is a good idea to check that the first and sixth strings sound like different versions of the same note.

Fourth fret

Sixth string

Fifth fret

You can tune your guitar using pitch pipes. The names of the notes of each string should be marked on the pipes.

An electronic tuner has a dial which tells you when each string is in tune.

You can use a tuning fork labeled E 329.6Hz. This produces a note you can tune your first or sixth string to.

Hold the tuning fork and hit one prong sharply on your knee to hear the note.

6th string note

5th string note

4th string note

This diagram shows you which note on the keyboard to play for each string.

3rd string note

2nd string note

1st string note

Middle C

READING MUSIC

If you want to get the most out of playing it is important to learn how to read music. It is also very useful if you want to start writing your own tunes and songs. Musical notes are written on a set of five lines called a staff (or stave). Some notes are written on the lines, and others in the spaces between them. How high or low a note sounds is called its pitch.

The higher the pitch, the higher up the staff it is written. Some notes are too high or too low to fit on the staff. These notes have extra, short lines above or below the staff. The name of each note depends on a sign at the beginning of the staff called a clef. The clef used for guitar music is called the treble clef. You can see the pitches and their names on the staff below.

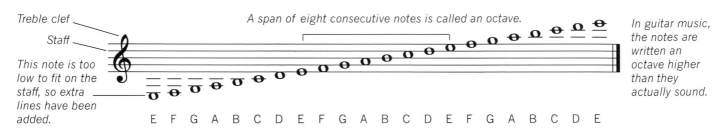

Treble clef

Staff

This note is too low to fit on the staff, so extra lines have been added.

A span of eight consecutive notes is called an octave.

In guitar music, the notes are written an octave higher than they actually sound.

E F G A B C D E F G A B C D E F G A B C D E

Finding the notes on your guitar

The diagrams below show you how to match notes on your guitar with notes on the staff. Practice finding a note, then looking at it on the staff.

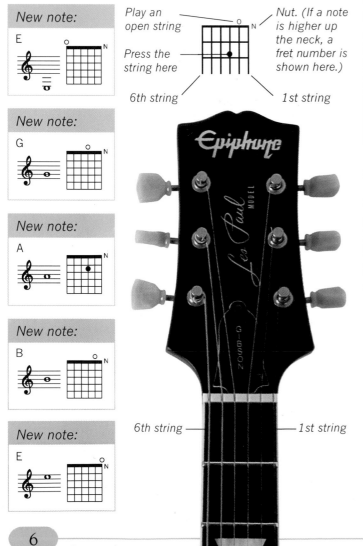

New note:

E

New note:

G

New note:

A

New note:

B

New note:

E

Play an open string

Press the string here

6th string

Nut. (If a note is higher up the neck, a fret number is shown here.)

1st string

6th string

1st string

How long notes last

As well as showing you the pitch of each note, music tells you how long notes last. Note lengths are measured in steady counts called beats. The shape of a note tells you how many beats it lasts for. You can see three of the most common note lengths below.

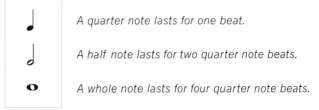

A quarter note lasts for one beat.

A half note lasts for two quarter note beats.

A whole note lasts for four quarter note beats.

Grouping notes together

When music is written down, it is divided up into small sections, called measures, by vertical lines called bar lines. Each measure contains the same number of beats. At the beginning of the music, a sign called a time signature tells you how many beats there are in each measure, and what kind of beats they are.

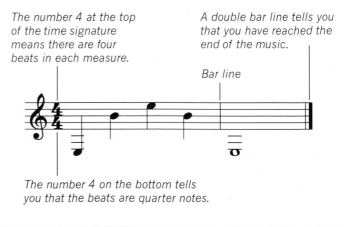

The number 4 at the top of the time signature means there are four beats in each measure.

A double bar line tells you that you have reached the end of the music.

Bar line

The number 4 on the bottom tells you that the beats are quarter notes.

TABLATURE

Tablature is another way of writing down guitar music, often used by rock guitarists. It uses six lines which represent the strings of a guitar (the top line is for the first string). Numbers on the lines tell you at which fret (or frets) to play. The tunes in this book are written in tablature, as well as on a staff. Try to read the music from the staff, but use the tablature to help you find the notes if you need to.

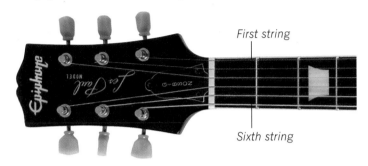

First string

Sixth string

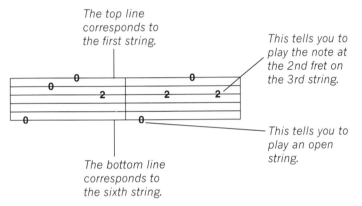

The top line corresponds to the first string.

This tells you to play the note at the 2nd fret on the 3rd string.

The bottom line corresponds to the sixth string.

This tells you to play an open string.

Jeff Beck was born in England, in 1944. He first became known when he replaced Eric Clapton (see page 3) in the Yardbirds, in 1965. For a short time Beck embarked on a solo career, producing the hit single *Hi Ho Silver Lining*. Later he formed his own band, the Jeff Beck group, featuring a variety of artists, including Rod Stewart.

City lights

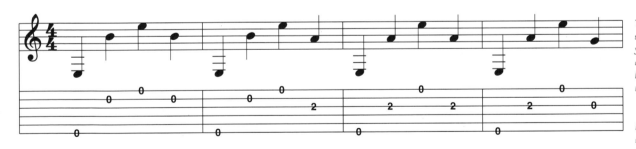

The time signature tells you there are four quarter note beats in each measure.

Play the tune very slowly at first, keeping a steady beat.

Practice until you can play it without any mistakes before going on to the next page.

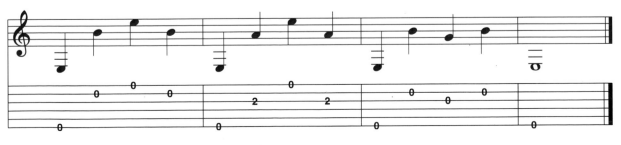

MAKING A GOOD SOUND

Try playing a note and, while the string is still sounding, rock your left hand as quickly as you can, either backward and forward, or from side to side.

The pitch of the note varies between the original pitch and one slightly higher. You may find this easier if you relax your left-hand thumb. This effect is called *vibrato*.

Sounds and silences

As well as sounds, music also contains silences. There are symbols called rests that tell you where there are silences, and how long they last. Three of the most common types of rests are shown on the right. When you see one in a tune, count the correct number of beats in your head before you play the next note.

A quarter rest lasts for one quarter note beat.

A half rest lasts for two quarter note beats.

A whole rest lasts for four quarter note beats. (This symbol is also used to show a rest lasting for a whole measure, whatever the time signature.)

Take a break

When an open-string note is followed by a rest, you need to stop the string from ringing on too long. After the correct number of beats, touch the strings with the side of your right hand to deaden the sound. This is called damping. You can find out more about damping on page 30.

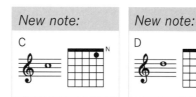

New note: C

New note: D

A wavy line above a note tells you to use vibrato.

To stop the Es at the beginning of each measure from ringing on too long, count the correct number of beats then damp the string.

Shorter notes

Some notes are shorter than a quarter note. An eighth note lasts for half a quarter note beat. Eighth notes can be joined together in groups of two, three or four. To count an eighth note rhythm, it helps to say "one-and two-and three-and four-and", instead of "one two three four".

One eighth note lasts for half a quarter note beat.

Two eighth notes last for one quarter note beat.

An eighth rest lasts for half a quarter note rest.

8

USING REVERB

To make tunes sound more interesting, you can use effects like reverberation (reverb). Reverb produces a series of echoes, which sound quickly one after the other. Some amplifiers have built-in reverb. If your amp has a reverb knob, try experimenting with different levels of reverb in the tunes you have learned so far. Listen carefully to the music to work out which level of reverb sounds best for each tune.

Echoes

Count very carefully. It might help to clap the rhythm before you start to play.

When you are sure of the notes, try playing this tune a little faster.

Born in the USA in 1960, **Steve Vai** took up the guitar at an early age. He studied at the Berklee School of Music with guitar teacher and performer Joe Satriani (see page 25). During the 1970s he played with Frank Zappa (see page 17) and the band Alcatrazz, later moving to the band Whitesnake. In 1990 he released his second solo album, *Passion and Warfare*, which is often thought of as a showcase for Vai's stunning technical skills.

Taking care of your guitar

Electric guitars are fragile instruments and need to be handled carefully. If you look after your instrument properly it will be much less likely to go wrong.

Checklist for taking care of your guitar

- When you finish playing, clean the strings, neck and body with a soft cloth and put your guitar back in its case.

- Keep your guitar away from too much heat. Make sure you do not leave it next to a radiator or in direct sunlight, even when it is in its case.

- If necessary, use a damp cloth to remove stains, but never use cleaning fluid unless it is recommended by the manufacturer or the shop where you bought the guitar.

LEARNING TUNES

It can take time to relate written notes to the notes on your guitar. The more you look at the music and try to play it, the easier it will become. The tunes in this book will help you to learn a little at a time. In the checklist on this page there are some tips to help you when you start to learn a new tune.

 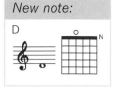

Using your left hand

You need to keep the fingernails of your left hand fairly short, so you can press the strings down using the very tips of your fingers. At first, your fingers may feel a little sore. Instead of playing for a long time once a week, practice often, for short amounts of time. As soon as your fingers begin to feel sore, stop playing and try again later.

Keep your fingertips upright, at right angles to the strings.

Checklist for learning tunes

- Look at the time signature. Remember, this tells you how many beats to count in each measure.

- Before starting to play, count the beats out loud, or in your head, and clap the rhythm at the same time.

- When you can do this, work out the notes and fit them to the rhythm. Try not to rush, and keep counting steadily.

- Don't worry if you can't do everything at once. Work through the music slowly and it will soon begin to make sense.

Red alert

Watch out for the rests in this tune. Keep counting the beats during the rests, just as you count them for the notes.

Try to read the notes on the staff, using the tablature to check your fingering if you need to.

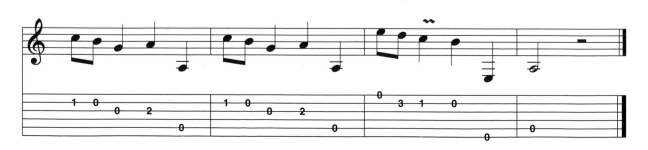

Using your right hand

If you want to play without using a pick, use your right-hand thumb and first three fingers. Play the lowest three strings with your thumb, and the highest three strings with your fingers. In guitar music, the letters *p*, *i*, *m* and *a* show you which right-hand finger to use for each string. On the right you can see which finger each of these letters stands for.

Your right-hand thumb and fingers are named after the first letter of the Spanish words for them.

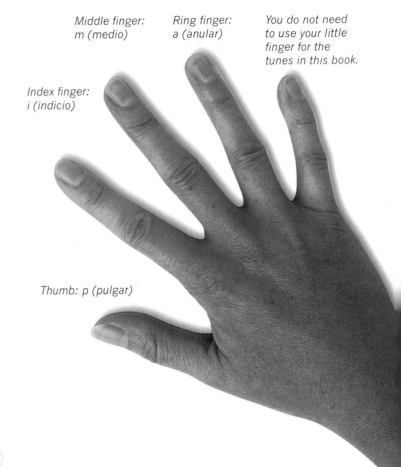

Middle finger:
m (medio)

Ring finger:
a (anular)

You do not need to use your little finger for the tunes in this book.

Index finger:
i (indicio)

Thumb: *p (pulgar)*

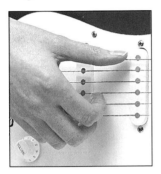

To play a string with your finger, rest your thumb on the sixth string, arching your hand slightly. Play the string with your fingertip, keeping your finger bent. It should push the string sideways, and end up above the strings, bent in toward the palm of your hand.

To play a string with your thumb, you make a circle shape in the air. Hold your thumb straight and push downward and outward. Finish with your thumb above the string. Make sure only your fingers and thumb move, not your whole arm.

Don't look back!

You could try playing this tune with a pick at first, then using your fingers to play the strings.

The letters only appear above the music the first time you play a sequence. Use the same fingering every time you see that sequence.

USING THE TREMOLO ARM

The tremolo arm (or whammy bar) alters the pitch of a note. As you move the tremolo arm up or down, the pitch also goes up or down. If your guitar does not have a tremolo arm, play the tunes on this page using vibrato.

This sign tells you to lift the tremolo arm.

This sign tells you to press the arm down.

If ½ appears above the sign, only move the arm slightly. The note you produce should be the same as the note one fret above or below the main note.

If Full appears above the sign, move the arm a little farther. The note you produce should be the same as the note two frets above or below the main note.

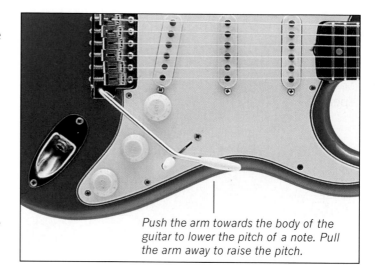

Push the arm towards the body of the guitar to lower the pitch of a note. Pull the arm away to raise the pitch.

Tied notes

A curved line between two notes on the same line or space of the staff is called a tie. Play the first note and hold it for the length of both notes added together. Don't play the second note separately.

A quarter note tied to another quarter note lasts for two quarter note beats.

Dotted notes

A dot after a note makes it one and a half times its normal length. So a dotted half note lasts for three quarter note beats, and a dotted quarter note lasts for one and a half quarter note beats.

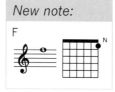

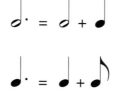

New note: F

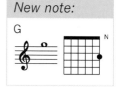

New note: G

Armed and dangerous

Notes played using the tremolo arm are written as tied notes, because only the first note is actually struck.

Move the tremolo arm in the rhythm shown by the notes.

If your tremolo only moves down, you can have it changed so it can move both ways. For extra advice, take it to a guitar shop.

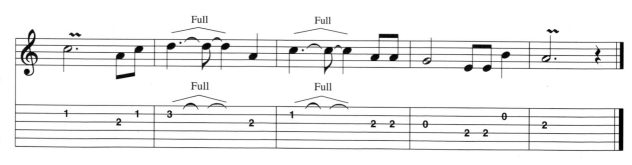

Repeats

A repeat sign tells you to play some of the music again. Repeat the music from the beginning, or from the previous repeat sign, if there is one. Ignore the repeat the second time you reach it.

Repeat from the beginning of the piece or from the previous repeat sign.

Repeat the music between these signs.

Second chance

Remember to play the first section of the music twice.

You only need to move the tremolo arm a small amount for this tune.

Born James Marshall Hendricks in 1942 in the USA, **Jimi Hendrix** was one of the most influential guitarists ever. In 1965 he formed his own band under the name Jimmy James and the Blue Flames, but it was when Chas Chandler (bass guitarist with the Animals) invited him to London that his most important band, the Jimi Hendrix Experience, was formed. Their first single, *Hey Joe*, an instant success, was closely followed by three more hit singles, including one of their most successful, *Purple Haze*. One of Hendrix's most memorable performances was at the Monterey Pop Festival in 1967, where he set his guitar alight before smashing it up on stage. This dramatic display made him a huge star.

SHARPS AND FLATS

A sharp sign (♯) before a note makes it a fret higher. A flat sign (♭) makes it a fret lower. These signs also affect any note later in the measure on the same line or space. Both of these signs are canceled out by a bar line, so a note in the next measure on the same line or space is not affected.

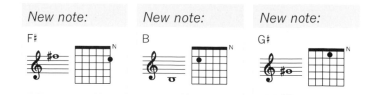

New note:
F♯

New note:
B

New note:
G♯

Scales

A scale is a special sequence of notes. Most music is based on scales. There are several different types of scales. The most common type is the major scale. A scale is named after the note on which it begins. For example, a major scale starting on G is called a G major scale. A piece of music based on a G major scale is said to be in the key of G major. You can see what this scale looks like below.

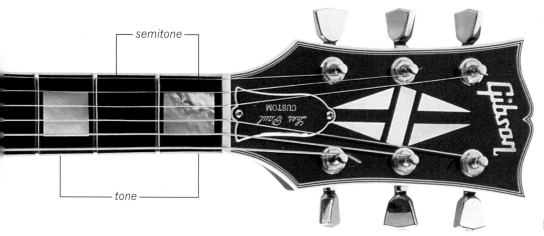

— semitone —

— tone —

A major scale contains two types of steps (or intervals) between the notes. These are called tones and semitones. On a guitar, there is a tone between any two notes that are two frets apart, and a semitone between any two notes that are one fret apart.

In a major scale, the tones and semitones always come in the same order: tone, tone, semitone, tone, tone, tone, semitone. In a G major scale, the semitones are between B and C, and between F♯ and G. All the other notes are a tone apart (see below).

G major scale

T = Tone
S = Semitone

T T S T T T S

Practicing scales

It is very important to practice scales when you are learning a musical instrument. It will help you to become familiar with the notes so you no longer have to search for them. This makes learning tunes a much easier task. Practice the G major scale below until you can play it fluently, without any mistakes.

G major scale

Use the same right-hand fingering throughout the scale.

PLAYING CHORDS

In guitar music you often have to play more than one note at a time. This is called playing chords. Chords are often used for accompanying a tune. Sometimes they are shown by letters above the staff, rather than being written out as separate notes. Major chords are based on major scales. A major chord consists of the first, third and fifth notes of the scale it is based on.

When you first play chords, position your left-hand fingers, then play each string separately to check that all the notes are sounding. Then run your thumb, or pick, across all the strings used for that chord, starting with the lowest. This is called strumming. Practice playing the E major chord below a few times before playing the next tune.

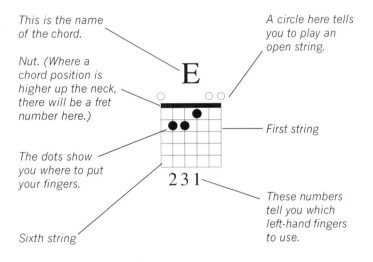

This is the name of the chord.

Nut. (Where a chord position is higher up the neck, there will be a fret number here.)

The dots show you where to put your fingers.

Sixth string

A circle here tells you to play an open string.

First string

These numbers tell you which left-hand fingers to use.

Checklist for playing chords

- Practice fingering each chord shape slowly at first. Play each string separately before strumming the whole chord.

- Try strumming a chord several times, until you can hear every note clearly. Then, remove your fingers and try again.

- When you are confident about the notes, try playing some chords and keeping a steady beat. Imagine there are four beats in each measure. It may help to play the first chord in each measure with a little more force than the others.

- You could choose a rhythm from a tune in this book. Then play some chords using that rhythm, to practice keeping in time. Chords are often used to accompany other people, so it is very important to keep a steady beat.

A step ahead

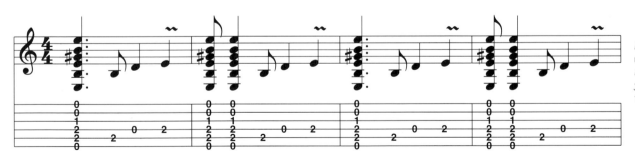

It might help to work out the rhythm before you play this tune.

MORE ABOUT CHORDS

In the key of G major there are three chords that will always sound good played one after the other. These are the chords starting on the first, fourth and fifth notes of the scale (G, C and D). You can play these chords in any order, but to play a sequence with a strong ending, finish by playing chord D, then G. You can make up a chord sequence using this three-chord trick in any key, by playing the chords starting on the first, fourth and fifth notes of the scale.

A cross above the nut tells you not to play that string.

Sixteenth notes

A sixteenth note is half as long as an eighth note. So two sixteenth notes last for one eighth note beat, and four sixteenth notes last for one quarter note beat. Sixteenth notes are often joined in groups by two lines.

One sixteenth note

Four sixteenth notes joined together

Sixteenth rest

Writing chords down

When a tune is made up entirely of chords, sometimes a special symbol (see below) is used, instead of writing out all the notes. The letter name of the chord is then written above the staff. You can check the notes in each chord by looking at the tablature.

Play a G chord until the letter above the staff changes.

Strumming

When you are playing chords, sometimes you strum downward (from the lowest note to the highest) and sometimes you strum upward (from the highest note to the lowest). There are signs in the music to tell you which way to strum.

This sign tells you to strum downward.

This sign tells you to strum upward.

Struck down

To end, play a G chord after the repeat sign.

On page 46 you can see which chords to use in some other keys.

You could try making up some tunes of your own using these three chords.

Use the signs telling you which way to strum as a guide, but feel free to change them so they are comfortable for you.

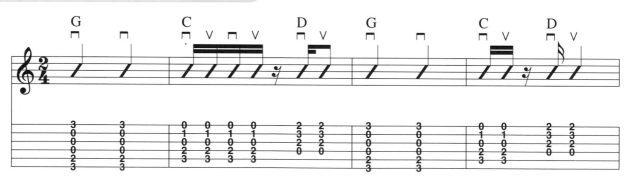

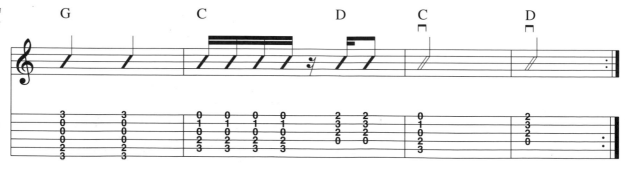

CHANGING STRINGS

Guitar strings do not last forever. Sometimes the sound becomes dull because the strings have lost their elasticity and they need to be replaced, or sometimes they just snap. When you change a string, start by loosening the old one gently. When you tighten a new string, keep your face well away in case the string breaks and lashes out. Never tighten a string above its correct pitch, as this can cause it to break. The pictures below show you how to restring your electric guitar.

1. Loosen the old string at the machine head, then release it from the bridge. If your guitar has a tailpiece, or a combined tailpiece and bridge, thread the new string through the hole in the tailpiece.

2. The strings on solid body electric guitars sometimes go right through the body. Loosen the old string, pull it out from the back, then thread the new one through to the front.

3. Pull the string up to the machine head. Thread the string through the hole in the capstan (the metal post), out toward the edge of the guitar. Leave about 5cm (2in) slack.

4. Start tightening the string by turning the machine head. As you do this, coil the string neatly around the capstan, toward the headstock. Coil the loose end around or snip it off.

5. If your guitar has a tremolo arm, you may have to thread the strings through the tremolo unit at the nut, then attach them to the machine heads in the usual way. The locking nut on the tremolo unit has to be tightened with an Allen key or a screwdriver after restringing. Make sure your guitar is properly in tune (see below) before tightening the locking nut.

Locking nut

Only tighten these when your guitar is properly in tune.

Tuning new strings

After changing your strings, tune them to the correct notes, wait for a short while, then pull each string away from the body a little. They will drop slightly in pitch. You need to do this two or three times, until the pitches stay the same when each string is pulled.

Frank Zappa was born in the USA in 1940, and died in 1993. Although he was not a mainstream artist, he had a large cult following and was highly respected by his fellow musicians. He released over fifty albums and more than 200 musicians recorded with him, or played with him live on stage. For a documentary film called 200 *Motels*, featuring Ringo Starr, he joined forces with the conductor, Zubin Mehta and the Los Angeles Philharmonic orchestra. He is also known for his bizarre album titles, such as *Lumpy Gravy*, *Burnt Weeny Sandwich* and *Weasels Ripped My Flesh*.

INTROS

If you want to start making up your own songs, start by thinking of different ways to begin. There are some suggestions for introductions to songs below. Try these first, then try making up some of your own. It is a good idea to listen to how other people start their songs. Listen to some of your favorite songs for ideas.

Naturals

A natural sign (♮) cancels a sharp or flat on the same line or space earlier in the measure. Sometimes the sign appears in the following measure, as a reminder.

Intro 1

Play this intro with a pick.

Try repeating each intro several times, perhaps even changing it slightly each time.

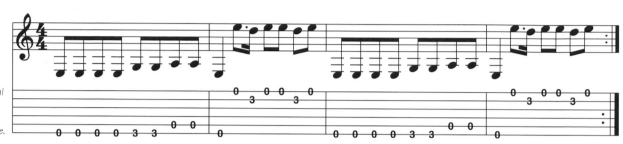

Intro 2

The second time you play this intro could be the start of a verse.

Intro 3

You could make up a melody line to go with this intro, by humming while you play.

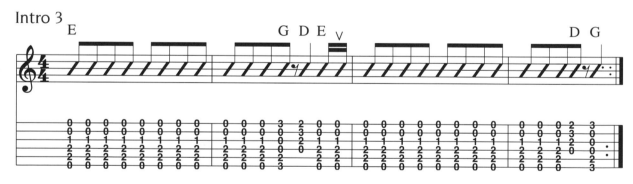

Playing loudly and quietly

There are signs in music that tell you how loudly or quietly to play. To play louder, strike the strings slightly harder, with your fingers more upright, or strike them harder with your pick.

ƒ   *Short for* forte, *which means "loudly"*

p   *Short for* piano, *which means "quietly"*

ƒƒ   *Short for* fortissimo, *which means "very loudly" (louder than* forte*)*

pp   *Short for* pianissimo, *which means "very quietly" (quieter than* piano*)*

mƒ   *Short for* mezzo forte, *which means "fairly loudly" (quieter than* forte*)*

mp   *Short for* mezzo piano, *which means "fairly quietly" (louder than* piano*)*

ENDINGS

Some songs fade out gradually and never really end, while others have a definite ending. If you are recording a song, it is easy to fade the music out when it reaches the end, but this does not always work so well if you are performing live. Below there are some examples of definite endings. They can all be played with the intros on page 18. When you can play them, try making up some of your own.

Ending 1

This ending is in the same style as the first intro. Try playing the intro, then the ending.

Play this with a pick.

Ending 2

Slow down in the last two measures of this ending.

If you feel adventurous, you could try making up some music to go in between the second intro and this ending.

Ending 3

You can play this ending with the third intro.

Born in 1952 in Northern Ireland, **Gary Moore** is one of Britain's most talented rock and blues guitarists. His first band, Skid Row, was formed in 1969 with vocalist and guitarist Phil Lynott. Lynott then started the band Thin Lizzy, of which Moore later became a member in 1974. After his success with Thin Lizzy, he embarked on a solo career in 1979, and soon after produced the hit record *Parisienne Walkways*. This was re-recorded and released again in 1993, and is still very popular, especially in Europe.

CHANGING POSITION

So far in this book, your left hand has been positioned so that your first finger is at the first fret, your second finger is at the second fret, and so on. This is called first position. When you play notes higher up the neck (toward the body), your first finger is placed at a higher fret.

For example, when you play in second position, your first finger is at the second fret, your second finger is at the third fret, and so on. Changing position makes some combinations of notes easier to play. Roman numerals above the staff tell you which position to play in (see below). In the next tune you start in third position (III), then move to second position (II), then first (I).

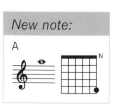

New note:

A

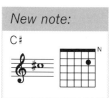

New note:

C♯

All change

Watch out for the ties. Count very carefully.

Think about which direction to strum for each chord. Make sure it feels natural.

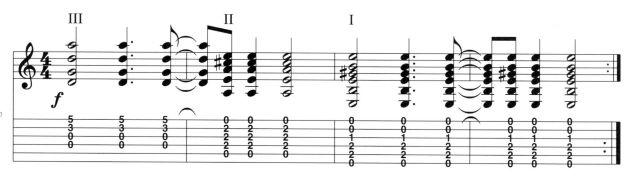

Practicing

If you practice carefully, the things you learn in this book will soon become much easier. Everyone has their own way of practicing, but there are some good general rules you can follow which will help you to get the most from your practice. Look at the checklist below for some useful advice.

Checklist for practicing

- Choose a time when you are not in a hurry, and you are not likely to be disturbed.

- Make sure you sit or stand in a comfortable position, with your arms and hands relaxed.

- Learn new tunes slowly at first, and work out the rhythm before you try playing the notes.

- Play a tune you already know well at the beginning of your practice. This will help you to warm up your fingers and to feel confident about your playing.

- Practice any difficult parts separately.

- Practicing a little each day is better than playing for a long time once a week.

BASS GUITAR

Most bass guitars have only four strings. These are tuned to the same notes as the four lowest strings of an ordinary electric guitar, but one octave lower. Most bands have a bass guitarist. The bass player usually follows the rhythm of the drums, giving the music a solid beat.

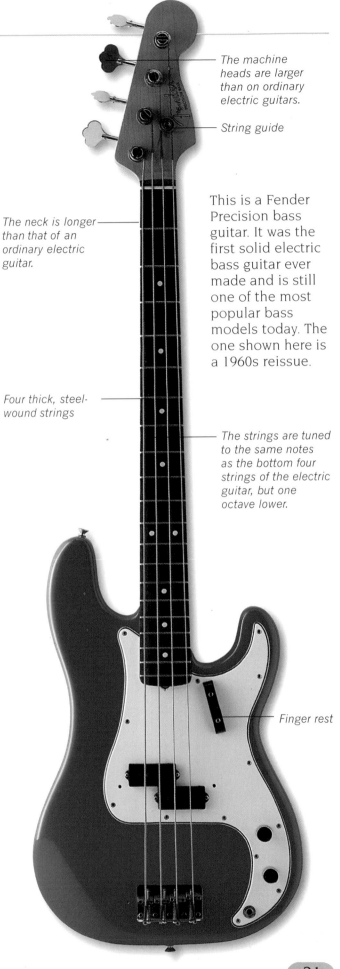

The machine heads are larger than on ordinary electric guitars.

String guide

The neck is longer than that of an ordinary electric guitar.

This is a Fender Precision bass guitar. It was the first solid electric bass guitar ever made and is still one of the most popular bass models today. The one shown here is a 1960s reissue.

Four thick, steel-wound strings

The strings are tuned to the same notes as the bottom four strings of the electric guitar, but one octave lower.

Finger rest

Stanley Clarke was born in 1951 in the USA. Originally he was a double bass player but, after taking up the electric bass guitar, he soon became a pioneer of jazz-rock. He created unusual sounds by slapping the strings instead of plucking them.

Tina Weymouth, born in 1950 in the USA, played bass guitar in the band Talking Heads. She was also a member of the Tom Tom Club, playing on tracks such as the 80's disco hit *Genius of Love*.

Born Gordon Matthew Sumner in England in 1951, **Sting** is famous, not only as a bass guitar player, but also as a songwriter and vocalist.

PLAYING RHYTHM GUITAR

Bands often have two guitarists, one to play the melodic sections, and one to keep a steady rhythm. The rhythm guitarist has to be able to change chords smoothly while keeping a steady beat. He or she also has to play loudly enough to be heard, without overpowering the melody.

Steady on

Try to change from one chord to the next as smoothly as possible.

Think about which direction to strum for each chord. Make sure it feels natural.

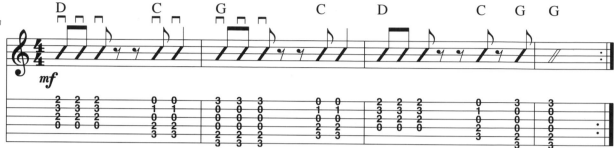

Power chords

Power chords are two-note chords, often used in rock music. You can keep the same shape with your left-hand fingers and move them up the neck to play different chords. They are named after the note you play with your left-hand first finger. Roman numerals above the chords tell you at which fret to put your first finger (I = first fret, III = third fret and V = fifth fret).

Power surge

Power chords are most effective when they are played with distortion. If your amp does not have this effect, you can buy a separate pedal to plug into your amp.

New note:
F

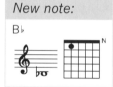

New note:
B♭

New note:
F

Slide your fingers along the neck, instead of lifting them off for each chord.

Hit the strings firmly with a pick to get a strong biting sound.

One of the leading rock bands of the 80s and early 90s was **Bon Jovi**. They developed a very distinctive style by combining typical heavy metal sounds with catchy pop songs, making their music accessible to a wider audience than most hard rock groups. Two of the band's first hit singles were *You Give Love a Bad Name*, and *Livin' on a Prayer*, from their million-seller album *Slippery When Wet*.

BARRE CHORDS

For some chords you need to put your first finger across all six strings. This is called using a barre. In *Final warning* below, keep your left-hand fingers in the same shape for each chord, moving them up or down the neck to change from one chord to another. Keep your finger straight, pressing firmly just behind the fret. A curved line on a chord diagram tells you to play a barre.

Final warning

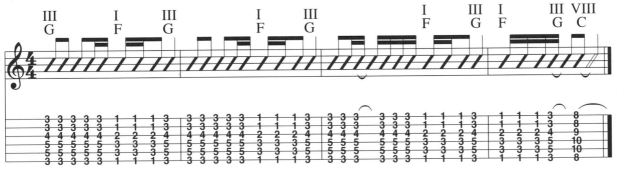

Work out which way to strum each chord. Then practice moving from one chord to another smoothly.

For some chords you need to make a barre with your third finger as well. Press the notes on the second, third and fourth strings all at the same time, by flattening your third finger across them. This is called a half barre. You need to use both types of barre chord in the tune below.

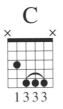

Attack!

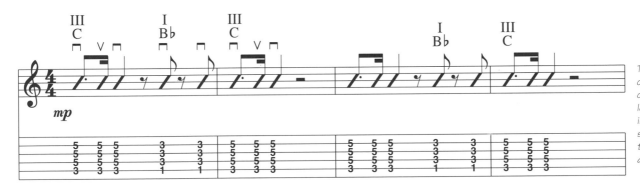

To change from one chord to the other, keep your left-hand fingers in the same shape and move them up or down the neck.

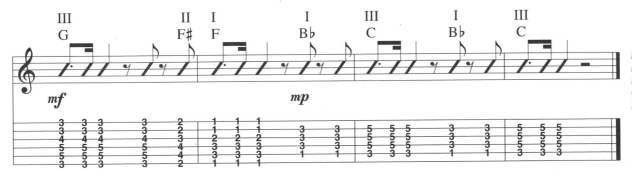

In the first two measures of this line, you play the first type of barre chord.

PLAYING LEAD GUITAR

The lead guitarist plays the melodic sections in a band. Sometimes this means following the vocal line of a song, but often it means playing a separate melody line alongside it. *Follow the leader*, below, is a typical lead guitar riff. Sometimes the lead guitarist uses special techniques to change the sound and make the music more interesting. You can find out about some of these techniques below the next tune.

New note:
B♭

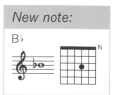

Follow the leader

Remember to play loudly.

This tune sounds best if you play it using a pick.

Hammer-on and pull-off

Hammer-on and pull-off are two of the most common techniques used by lead guitarists. You hammer-on by playing a note, then pressing down very hard on another fret on the same string, without striking the string again. Pull-off by playing a string, then pulling your finger off sideways so it pulls the string. In the music in this book, a curved line between two notes tells you when to do this. The letter H above or below the curved line means hammer-on, and the letter P above or below the line means pull-off.

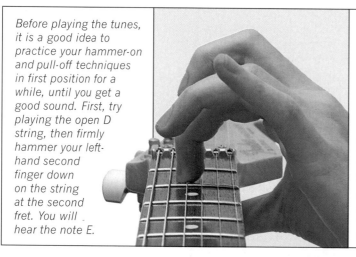

Before playing the tunes, it is a good idea to practice your hammer-on and pull-off techniques in first position for a while, until you get a good sound. First, try playing the open D string, then firmly hammer your left-hand second finger down on the string at the second fret. You will hear the note E.

Play the note E (at the second fret on the D string), then pull your second finger off sideways so it pulls the string. The D will sound again. Try using these techniques on other strings, to practice doing them smoothly. Before you try the tune on the opposite page, practice playing the hammer-on and pull-off sections.

Eddie Van Halen was born in Holland in 1957. After moving to California in 1968, he began to learn the drums, while his brother Alex started to play the guitar. After swapping instruments one day, Eddie found that he had a real flair for the guitar. With Alex now on drums, they formed the band Van Halen, along with David Lee Roth. One of the band's most successful singles was *Jump*. Eddie Van Halen also played the solo on the Michael Jackson song *Beat it*.

Lead guitar rhythms

Lead guitar rhythms are often complicated to read. This is because the emphasis is rarely on the main beats of the measure. (The main beats in 4/4 are the first and third beats.) It is a good idea to work out the rhythm carefully before playing the tune below. If you find it particularly difficult to work out the rhythm, try playing it without the ties at first. Then add them in later, when you are more confident of the rhythm.

Keep on running

Sometimes there are notes at the beginning of a piece that don't make up a full measure. These are called pick-up notes. The beats in the first and last measures add up to one complete measure.

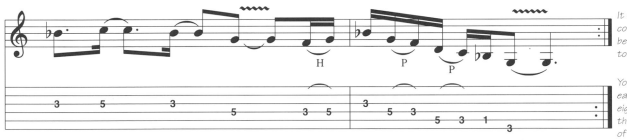

It may help to count to three before you start to play.

You might find it easier to count in eighth notes for this tune, instead of quarter notes.

Joe Satriani was born in 1957 in the USA. He is perhaps best known as a teacher, though he has played with many renowned guitarists and released a number of flashy solo albums. His technical skills have earned him an excellent reputation, and he is frequently asked to play with fellow artists, such as Mick Jagger, and the band Deep Purple.

Led Zeppelin was one of the most successful rock groups of the 70s. With massive hits, such as *Whole Lotta Love* and *Stairway to Heaven*, their music will be remembered for many years to come. Their lead guitar player, **Jimmy Page**, born in 1944 in England, has been a great inspiration to many later heavy metal guitarists.

MORE SCALES

You have already played the scale of G major (see page 14). Below you can see some more of the most common major scales. If you can play scales fluently, without any mistakes, you will find it easier to start making up your own songs. Practice the scales below until you can play them smoothly and evenly. Once you are sure of the notes, you could use them to try making up some music of your own.

(see page 14)

New note:

Key signatures

Sometimes there are sharp (♯) or flat (♭) signs at the beginning of the music, just after the treble clef. When you see one or more sharps or flats at the start of a staff, this is called a key signature. It tells you to play certain notes sharp or flat throughout the piece.

For example, if there is an F sharp in the key signature, you play every F in the piece as F sharp. If there is a B flat in the key signature, you play every B as B flat. Key signatures make music easier to read, because they prevent having to write out lots of flats or sharps.

C major scale

When you are sure of the notes, try playing these scales a little faster.

F major scale

This key signature tells you to play B flats throughout the scale.

D major scale

Play F sharps and C sharps all the way through.

ARPEGGIOS

Arpeggios are based on scales. The notes of an arpeggio are the first, third, fifth and eighth notes of a scale, played one after the other. There are some arpeggios below, in the same keys as the scales you have learned so far.

G major arpeggio

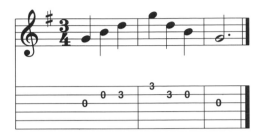

Arpeggios are useful if you want to start writing your own music.

C major arpeggio

Try mixing parts of an arpeggio with parts of a scale. Make sure you use a scale and arpeggio which are in the same key.

D major arpeggio

Remember to look at the key signature.

F major arpeggio

When you can play these arpeggios fluently, try playing them faster.

Bonnie Raitt was born in the USA in 1949. As well as being a very accomplished electric guitar player, she is also widely thought of as one of the best female singers of the seventies and eighties. Her emotional singing voice, and her blues and folk guitar sound, make her music easy to recognize.

Born in America in 1954, **Pat Metheny** is one of the most versatile electric guitarists of our time, particularly in the fields of jazz and rock.

SOLOS

Sometimes the lead guitarist in a band plays a solo. Most guitarists see this as a chance to show off their skills as a player. Solos are often based on scales and arpeggios. So, if you want to play flashy solos, it is very important to learn scales. There are some examples of guitar solos below. When you can play the scales and arpeggios on pages 26 and 27, you could try making up some of your own solos.

Solos are often played higher up the neck of the guitar (closer to the body), because of the different sound this produces. This means that some of the notes you have learned so far may need to be played in a different position. Remember, you can check to see which string and fret to use for each note by looking at the tablature.

When you can play the scales and arpeggios on pages 26 and 27, you could try making up some of your own solos.

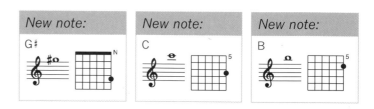

New note:	New note:	New note:
G♯	C	B

Triplets

A triplet sign tells you to play three notes in the time of two. Triplets are marked by a figure 3 above or below a group of three notes (in *Firefly* they are eighth ntoes). If there are lots of triplets in a tune, sometimes only the first few are marked with a figure 3. After this, the word *simile* (or *sim.*) tells you to play triplets for the rest of the piece.

Firefly

The word "simile" tells you to continue playing triplets and hammer-on and pull-off in the same way.

For the second measure, try putting your right-hand first finger on the first fret of the first string. This technique is often used by guitarists to add variety.

Try playing this faster when you are sure of the notes.

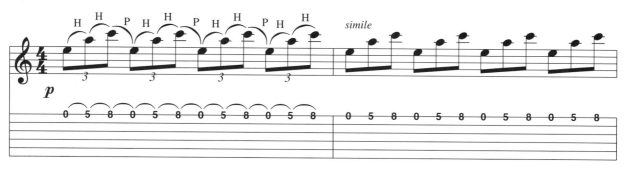

Moving on

Check the tablature in this tune, to make sure you are playing the notes in the correct position.

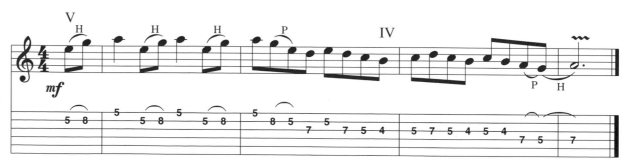

28

- When you play a solo you are usually the center of attention, so try to make your solos as interesting as possible. Always make sure they fit in with the song, though.

- Only use notes and techniques you feel confident about playing.

- Keep them short, to hold the listener's attention.

Ry Cooder, born in America in 1947, is one of the great masters of electric guitar. He is renowned for his wide variety of styles, ranging from calypso to folk, making him a highly sought-after session musician. As well as performing on albums for bands like The Rolling Stones (see page 36) and Randy Newman, he has also worked on film soundtracks.

Brian May was born in England in 1947. His unique style of guitar playing and memorable solos have earned him admiration and respect among millions of budding guitarists. Along with his friends Freddie Mercury, Roger Taylor and John Deacon, he formed the supergroup Queen. One of the most striking aspects of Queen's music, and of Brian May's guitar playing, is the use of multi-layered studio effects. Using these effects he has developed a style which is instantly recognizable. The guitar he uses, which he built himself, is now mass produced and widely available in guitar shops.

Born in the USA, **Stevie Ray Vaughn** (1954-1990) has been an inspiration to many electric guitarists. Heavily influenced by the music of Cream (see page 3) and Jimi Hendrix (see page 13), Vaughn was an extremely gifted blues-rock guitarist. After hearing him play at the 1982 Montreux Jazz Festival, David Bowie hired him to play on his album, *Let's Dance.*

PLAYING IN DIFFERENT STYLES

The electric guitar can be used to play many different types of music. Over the next few pages there are some tunes in styles such as funk, jazz, blues and reggae. Learning to play in a variety of different styles is very useful. It will broaden your knowledge of music and improve your technical skills. It is also helpful if you want to play in a band, or start writing your own songs.

Born in 1943 in the USA, **George Benson** has been highly regarded in the fields of jazz and soul for more than twenty-five years. Although he is now perhaps more widely known as a soul singer, he has often been referred to as one of the world's greatest guitarists.

Left-hand damping

On page 8 of this book you learned how to damp the strings with your right hand, to deaden the sound. You can also damp the strings using your left hand. To do this, keep your fingers on the strings, but release the pressure from them. Damped notes are written as Xs on the staff. Check the tablature for the finger positions.

Interference

The tune below is in a style known as funk. The emphasis is not always on the main beats, which makes the music very rhythmic and energetic. This off-beat rhythm is known as syncopation.

Remember to damp the strings where you see an X. This will add to the rhythmic effect.

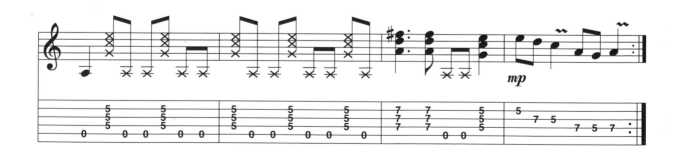

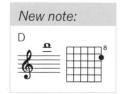

New note:

D

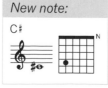

New note:

C♯

New note:

F♯

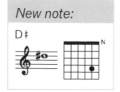

New note:

D♯

New note:

D♯

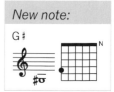

New note:

G♯

JAZZ GUITAR

Jazz guitarists use very distinctive chords. For the next tune, check the tablature for your finger positions. The A sharp in measures 4 and 12 uses the same fingering as B flat (see page 24). Both notes sound the same. Notes which have different names, but sound the same, are called enharmonics. You can see some other notes like this on page 46.

The slide sign

The sign on the right tells you to slide up to a note. Do this by striking a note on a lower fret, then sliding your left-hand finger up to the fret for the main note, without playing the string again.

Missing pieces

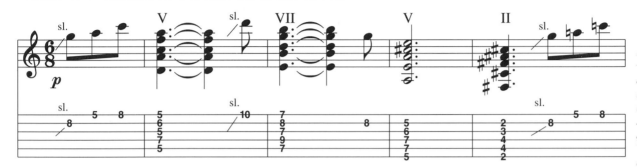

In 6/8 time there are six eighth note beats in each measure, arranged in two groups of three. You can either count in eighth notes or dotted quarter notes, with two dotted quarter notes in each measure.

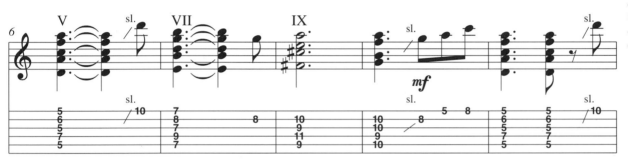

The first note of this tune is at the eighth fret of the second string. Try sliding up to this from the sixth fret of the same string.

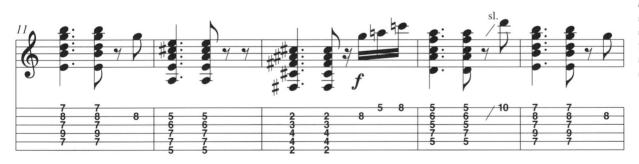

BLUES GUITAR

Blues music developed in the late 19th century in America. Early blues musicians played acoustic guitars to accompany themselves singing, but today most blues bands use electric guitars.

String-bending

This technique is often used by blues guitarists to add expression to the music. Play a note, and, as soon as it sounds, bend the string by pushing it across the fretboard with your left finger (see below). This alters the pitch of the note. A curved arrow after a note shows you where to play a bend.

 This tells you to bend the note up by one semitone, then return to the original pitch.

This tells you to bend the note up by a full tone, then return to the original pitch.

For notes on the top three strings, bend toward the sixth string.

For notes on the bottom three strings, bend toward the first string.

Born in 1925 in the USA, **B. B. King** is one of the most influential figures in blues guitar music. One of his earliest hits, *Woke up this Morning*, is still one of the best known blues songs today. Even after his success in the recording studio, King still toured constantly, performing up to 340 gigs a year. During his live performances he can often be heard talking to his guitar, whom he calls Lucille.

Back street blues

In 12/8 time there are twelve eighth note beats in each measure, arranged in four groups of three. You can either count in eighth notes or dotted quarter notes, with four dotted quarter notes in each measure.

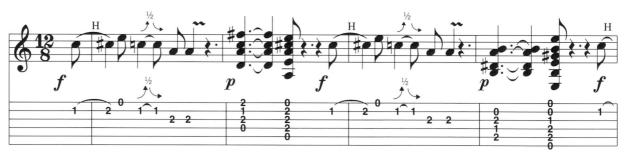

Before guitars were amplified, it was often difficult to hear them in a band. This is because they were not as loud as some of the other instruments, such as the drums. During the 1920s, guitar makers began to experiment with using pick-ups on ordinary acoustic guitars, to make them louder.

Rickenbacker twelve-string

The first solid body electric guitar was made by Rickenbacker in 1931. To amplify the sound, it used a simple pick-up made from two large magnets. Later, along with other manufacturers, Rickenbacker began to make guitars with twelve strings.

Fender Telecaster

Later, Leo Fender began to experiment with smaller pick-ups. By 1948 he had produced the Fender Broadcaster. This was later re-named the Fender Telecaster, to avoid confusion with another product of the same name.

Gibson Les Paul Special

At around the same time, Les Paul was also experimenting with amplified guitars. Later, he joined forces with a guitar manufacturer, Gibson, producing a range of Gibson Les Paul guitars, many of which are still popular today.

REGGAE

Reggae originated in Jamaica during the 1960s. The unusual guitar rhythms in reggae are created by damping the strings on certain beats of the measure This gives the music its character. Try playing the tune below using the left-hand damping technique explained on page 30.

Am

A small m tells you this is a minor chord (based on a minor scale). In minor scales, the tones and semitones are arranged differently.

2 3 1

D7

The number 7 tells you that, as well as the first, third and fifth notes of the scale, this chord also includes the seventh note.

2 1 3

Rising damp

Remember to damp the strings where there are Xs in the music.

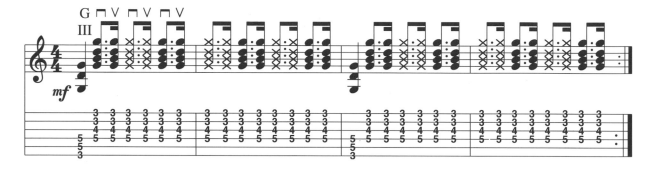

Dread café

Practice fingering the chords on their own before playing this tune.

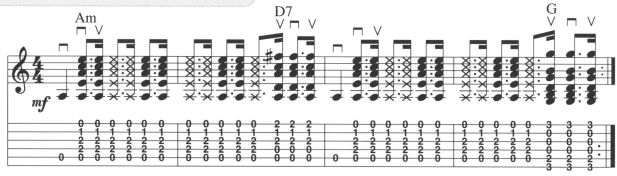

Nesta Robert Marley (1945-1981), better known as **Bob Marley,** was born in Jamaica. He is probably the most famous reggae artist in history, achieving international stardom with his group, Bob Marley and the Wailers, originally known as The Wailing Wailers. Although the group based their style on American pop music, their songs combine both rock and African themes. Later, they also incorporated other styles, such as blues, soul and funk, into their music. With this combination of sounds, and with the lyrics often being heavily influenced by politics, their music is very distinctive. Among their most successful hits are *Get up, Stand up, I Shot the Sheriff* and *No Woman, no Cry.*

DIFFERENT TYPES OF ELECTRIC GUITARS

There are lots of different types of electric guitars. Over the years, guitar manufacturers have experimented with guitar designs, trying to produce instruments which are distinctive to look at, as well as to play. You can see some of the most popular designs below.

Gibson Flying V solid electric

In an attempt to modernize their designs in the 1950s, Gibson came up with the Flying V. It is still made today.

Hofner Violin guitar

In the 1960s, another manufacturer, Hofner, produced a guitar in the shape of a violin.

Vox Phantom twelve-string

Like Gibson, other manufacturers were trying to bring their designs up to date by changing the shape of their guitars.

Kramer Baretta solid electric

Some guitar makers have experimented with producing a distinctive sound. Kramer electric guitars are particularly popular with heavy metal guitarists.

GUITAR BANDS

During the 1960s, guitar bands (bands whose music was made up mostly of guitars with percussion) were extremely popular. With the success of bands like The Beatles, more and more bands followed this style of music. The 1990s has seen a huge revival of the guitar band, with groups such as Nirvana (see page 43), Blur and R.E.M. achieving great success. You can find out about some of these bands below.

Emerging during the 60s in England, **The Beatles** were perhaps the most successful band in history.

The Rolling Stones were one of the greatest rock 'n' roll bands to hit the pop scene in the 60s and 70s.

The Sex Pistols had a huge impact on rock music during the 70s, with their punk style inspiring many other bands.

One of the leading beat groups in Britain in the 60s was **The Kinks.**

The Clash made a big impression in the 70s, with their political lyrics and tough, punk rock image.

Starting up in the mid-90s, **Supergrass** achieved great success with its single, *Alright*.

During the 90s, **Radiohead** has gained much critical acclaim with its album, *The Bends*.

The American guitar band, **Living Colour**, was popular during the mid-80s and 90s.

R.E.M. has been one of the most popular American rock groups of the late 80s and the 90s.

The UK band **Blur** has influenced many aspiring musicians during the 90s.

After releasing *Definitely Maybe*, which became the fastest selling debut album of the 1990s, **Oasis** achieved instant fame.

Investigator

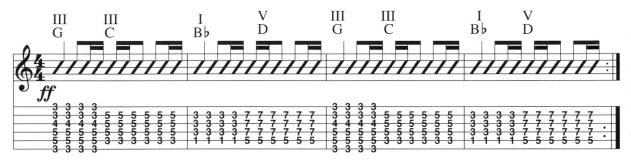

Try to work out which way to strum each chord in this tune. Find a strumming pattern which you feel comfortable with.

Hidden agenda

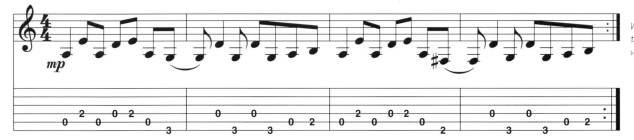

Watch out for the tied notes. Count very carefully.

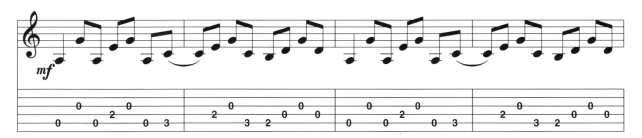

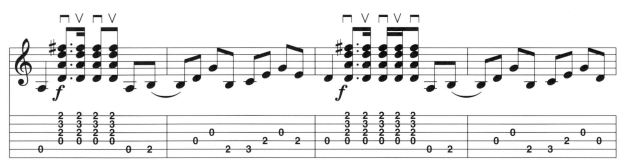

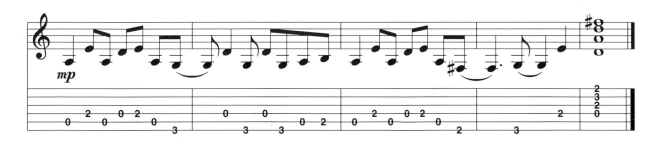

Making up music as you play is called improvising. Bands often improvise by choosing a sequence of chords, then improvising tunes or rhythms over it. Try improvising using the three-chord sequence described on page 16. Choose notes for the tune from the major scale starting on each chord note. At first, not every note you play will sound good with the chords. It takes time to learn which notes fit best, but the more you listen and experiment, the easier improvising becomes.

Recording your own music

One of the most important things to consider when you are making your own recording is where to do it. When you play a musical instrument, the sound is reflected from certain surfaces, such as walls or ceilings. When this happens, a slight echo can sometimes be heard. This is known as acoustics. Some rooms have better acoustics than others.

Checklist for recording your own music

- A room which has little, or no, echo can deaden the sound of an instrument, whereas a room with too much echo may blur the sound, so individual notes are not always clear.

- When you are choosing a room for your recording, look at the surfaces around you. Soft surfaces will soak up the sound, but hard surfaces will make the sound bounce off and echo.

- Listen to the sound carefully to decide whether a room is suitable.

- Try recording in some different rooms. Listen to the recordings to work out what the differences are. Then decide upon the sort of sound you are looking for, and try to match it to a recording.

- You should also consider other factors, such as background noise. Any noise outside the room will be picked up by a microphone, even if you are unaware of it.

Adapting a tune

Another way to invent new tunes is to adapt one you already know. Try playing some of the tunes in this book, and then experiment with changing notes or rhythms. Be as adventurous as you like. This is one of the best ways of finding out what sounds good, and developing your own style.

In a professional recording studio, a producer, or engineer, controls the sound levels at a mixing desk and decides if more takes are needed.

Using effects

Many guitarists use effects units to alter the sound of their instruments. These are usually plugged in between the guitar and the amplifier. They change the sound by altering the signal from the pick-ups. Most units have a footswitch to turn the effect on and off. There may also be other controls to vary the level or speed of the effect. On some units, the harder the pedal is pressed, the more intense the effect becomes.

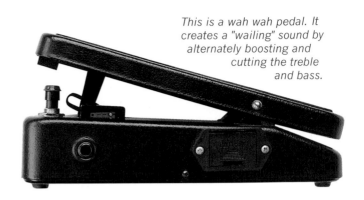

This is a wah wah pedal. It creates a "wailing" sound by alternately boosting and cutting the treble and bass.

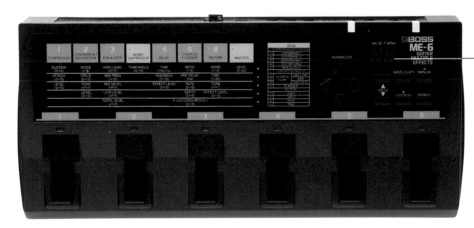

A multi-effects unit has several different effects built into one box. Single effects or combinations of effects can be selected by pressing the foot switches.

The digital display shows which effects have been selected.

A distortion pedal. Distortion is one of the most common guitar effects. It can make the sound fuzzy and muffled, or loud and piercing.

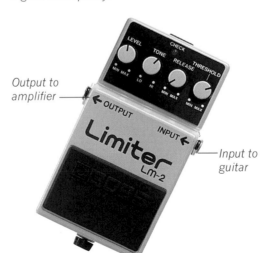

A limiter. This unit limits the amount of feedback and distortion to help maintain a good tone quality.

Output to amplifier

Input to guitar

With the turbo overdrive unit you can create a wide variety of distortion effects, from slightly fuzzy, to harsh heavy metal sounds.

Controls alter the tone, volume and the level of the effect.

Soundproofing

You may wish to soundproof a room to record your music. If you want to play without headphones, you may also wish to soundproof a room to avoid disturbing other people. Professional soundproofing is expensive, but a room with double glazing and heavy curtains will help to reduce noise coming into and out of a room. Sealing any gaps around doors and windows will help too.

HARMONICS

Harmonics are clear, bell-like notes made by touching a string lightly instead of pressing it down. You can only play harmonics at certain frets (the 4th, 5th, 7th, 9th and 12th). Try playing a harmonic at the twelfth fret on the sixth string. Gently touch the string, right over the fret, but don't press down. Play the string, then immediately lift your left-hand finger off the string to let the note ring. A harmonic is written as a diamond-shaped note with the word *Harm.* above it.

New note:

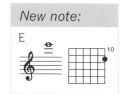

E

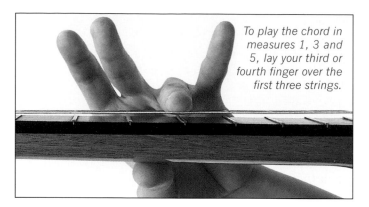

To play the chord in measures 1, 3 and 5, lay your third or fourth finger over the first three strings.

Distant chimes

Keep the same shape with your left-hand fingers for all the barre chords.

This tune will sound better with no distortion or reverb.

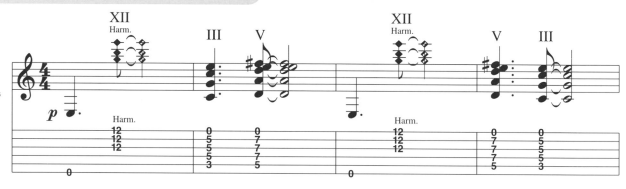

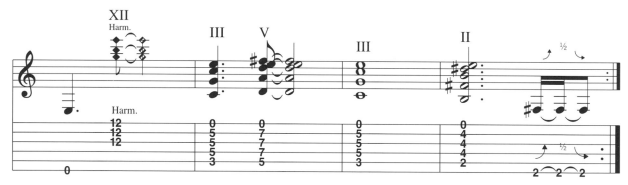

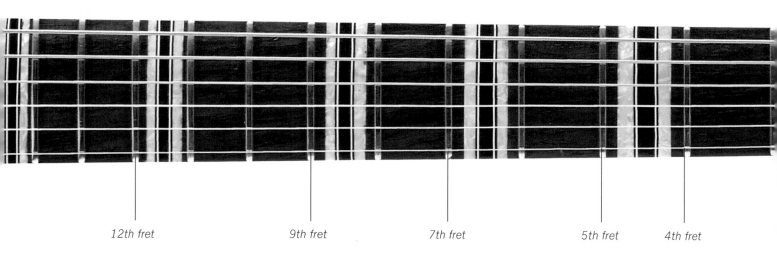

12th fret   9th fret   7th fret   5th fret   4th fret

TUNING WITH HARMONICS

One of the most accurate methods of tuning your guitar is to use harmonics. This is because harmonics produce a very clear sound. First tune your sixth string using one of the methods described on page 5. Then follow the steps below.

1. Play the harmonic at the fifth fret on the sixth string. Then, straight away, play the harmonic at the seventh fret on the fifth string. You can then hear both notes at the same time. Tune your fifth string so the harmonics are exactly the same.

2. Next play the harmonic at the fifth fret on the fifth string and the harmonic at the seventh fret on the fourth string. Tune the fourth string so the harmonics are the same.

3. Then play the harmonic at the fifth fret on the fourth string and the harmonic at the seventh fret on the third string. Tune the third string so the harmonics are the same.

4. To tune the second string, play the harmonic at the seventh fret on the sixth string. Then tune the second string to this note by playing an open string.

5. Finally, tune the first string by playing the harmonic at the fifth fret on the second string and the seventh fret on the first string.

Practicing harmonics

Harmonics can be difficult at first. Remember to lift your left-hand finger as soon as you have played the string. A good way to practice harmonics is to lay your third or fourth finger over all the strings, and then try to play all six harmonics.

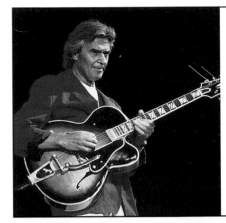

John McLaughlin was born in England in 1942. He became highly respected as an electric guitarist during the 1970s, after developing a unique style of playing which combined jazz with Indian music.

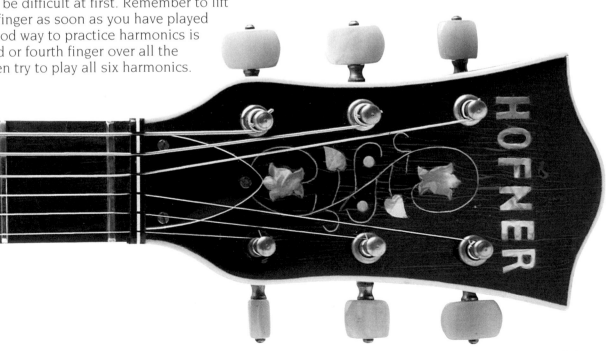

Poison Ivy, born Kirsty Marlana Wallace, is the lead guitarist with the American band, The Cramps, famous for their outrageous stage shows.

HOW TO WRITE A SONG

There are lots of ways to start writing your own songs. You can start by making up a tune or a chord sequence, or by writing some lyrics. Improvising (see page 38) is always a good way to start. When you have made up a tune or rhythm of your own, or found a chord sequence you like, try using it as the basis for composing a longer piece or a song. On these two pages there are some suggestions for how to do this. Follow the steps carefully, spending plenty of time thinking of ideas and experimenting with them.

Improvising (see page 38)

Thinking of ideas

Anything from a picture to a mood can be a starting point for writing your own music. Try lots of different ideas. The more you try, the more fun improvising becomes. When you find something you particularly like, write it down, or record it on a cassette, so you can remember it. Look at the tips below, then try making up some music of your own.

Checklist for thinking of ideas

- Listen to different types of music for ideas. Think about what sorts of sounds or rhythms you like best, and what you don't like too.

- Try writing new theme tunes for television programs you like. Think about which sounds and rhythms seem to fit with their stories or subjects.

- Think about different types of music. Why does dance music sound different from film music, jingles or ballads, for instance?

- Try to express some strong feelings in a tune. Think about what makes a cheerful tune sound different from a sad one.

Born John Maher in England in 1963, **Johnny Marr** played lead guitar in the 80s band The Smiths. While Steven Patrick Morrisey wrote the lyrics for the songs, Marr's highly inventive guitar parts gave the music a unique sound.

The Artist (formerly known as Prince) was born Prince Rogers Nelson in the USA in 1960.

He is one of the most creative, yet controversial, songwriters of the 80s and 90s.

Pete Townsend was born in England in 1945. He has been involved in music for most of his life, but it was with The Who that he gained his fame, both as a songwriter and a guitarist. One of his most successful projects was the rock opera *Tommy*.

Born in England in 1958, **Paul Weller** has been writing hit records for more than 20 years, first as the lead singer with The Jam, then The Style Council, and more recently as a solo artist. One of his most popular solo tracks is the sixties-style song *Uh Huh, Oh Yeh*, a hit single in the early 90s.

Starting with a tune

If you have composed a tune you like, you could try to find some chords that go with it, or make up a bass line to play at the same time. Keep listening until you find something you like. Then try to develop the tune, by changing a few notes, or playing it higher or lower. It is a good idea to write down the chord names or notes, to help you remember them.

Starting with some chords

If you have made up a chord sequence, try recording it, then play it back and improvise some tunes while you are listening to it. Try to find a melody line which sounds good with the chords you have chosen. You could add a separate bass line too. Use a chord sequence from a tune in this book, if you like.

Thinking about structure

A good structure will help your music to make sense. Think carefully about how to start and end your song. Try to begin with something interesting, to catch the listener's attention. Think about how many times you can repeat a tune or chord sequence before it begins to sound boring. Add variety by playing the same theme in slightly different ways. Listen to the various effects and moods you create. If you have written some lyrics, make sure the words fit comfortably with the melody and the general style of the music.

Checklist for adding variety

- Play the music an octave higher or lower, or start on a different note.

- Try playing your music faster or slower. This may make it sound very different.

- Experiment with sounds and rhythms. Some rhythms may sound better if you play the music at a different speed.

- Try adjusting the volume control so the sounds are much louder or quieter. Does this change the mood of the music?

- Change some of the notes in the tune when you repeat it, or change the chords that go with it.

- Try alternating two tunes. Make the tunes contrast with each other, for example in volume or speed.

- Use different effects pedals. Think about whether the music sounds better with or without distortion, or reverb.

Kurt Cobain (1967-1994) was the lead singer and guitarist for the American grunge band, Nirvana. Grunge music is a cross between punk and heavy metal, often using powerful distortion effects. One of the band's most popular singles was *Smells like Teen Spirit*.

PLAYING IN A BAND

On these two pages there is some music for you to play with other people. If you know someone who plays keyboards, the chords above the rhythm guitar part can be used by them as a guide. If you know anyone who plays the drums, you could ask them to play along too. Ask them to play a standard rock beat.

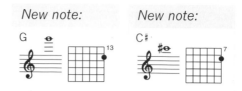

New note: G

New note: C#

Silent running (rhythm guitar part)

If you don't know anyone else who plays guitar, or bass guitar, you could record the rhythm guitar part, then play the lead guitar part along with it.

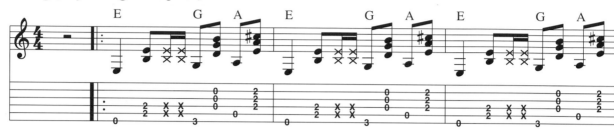

Make sure your instruments are in tune with each other. Play the same note and listen to hear if each note sounds the same. If you are playing with a keyboard player, all tune your instruments to the keyboard.

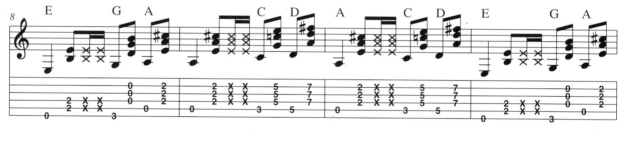

Silent running (lead guitar part)

A number 4 over a whole rest tells you to count four measures rest. Count very carefully to make sure you come in at the right time.

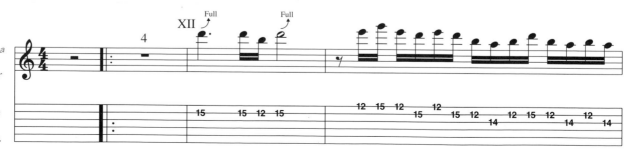

44

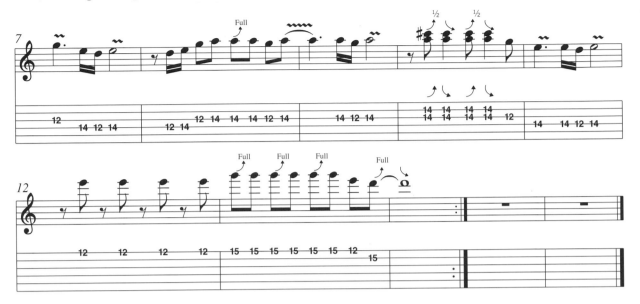

Silent running (bass guitar part)

If you don't know anyone who has a bass guitar, you could try playing this part on the bottom four strings of an ordinary electric.

FINGERING CHART

Below you can see the finger positions for all the notes on your electric guitar. Where two notes are shown on the same fret, these are enharmonics (see page 31).

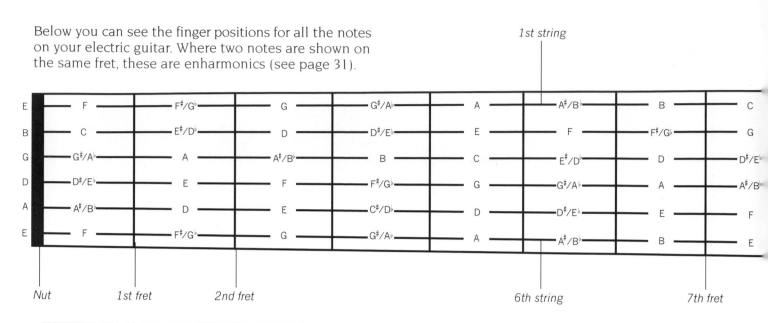

1st string

6th string

Nut *1st fret* *2nd fret* *7th fret*

Musical symbols key

The key below explains all the musical symbols used in this book. The page numbers shown in brackets are the pages where each sign first appears. If you want to find out more about these symbols and how to play the techniques described below, refer to the page shown in brackets.

~ This sign tells you to use vibrato (page 8).

⌃ This tells you to lift the tremolo arm (page 12).

⌄ This tells you to press the tremolo arm (page 12).

½ Lift the tremolo arm slightly, to produce a note a semitone higher than the main note (page 12).

Full Push the tremolo arm so the note you produce is a tone lower than the main note (page 12).

⫣ This tells you to play a chord. A letter above this sign tells you which chord to play (page 16).

⊓ This tells you to strum downward (page 16).

V This tells you to strum upward (page 16).

f This is short for forte, which means "loudly" (page 18).

p This is short for piano, which means "quietly" (page 18).

ff This is short for fortissimo, which means "very loudly" (page 18).

pp This is short for pianissimo, which means "very quietly" (page 18).

mf This is short for mezzo forte, which means "fairly loudly" (page 18).

mp This is short for mezzo piano, which means "fairly quietly" (page 18).

H Hammer-on. Play a note, then press down hard on another fret, without striking the string again (page 24).

P Pull-off. Play a string, then pull your finger sideways so it pulls the string (page 24).

✗ Play the note damped. To do this, keep your finger on the string, but release the pressure (page 30).

sl Slide up to a note. Strike a note on a lower fret, then slide your finger up the neck for the main note (page 31).

½ This tells you to bend the note up by one semitone, then return to the original pitch (page 32).

Full This tells you to bend the note up by a full tone, then return to the original pitch (page 32).

Harm. This tells you to play a harmonic (page 40).

Notes which have different names, but sound the same, are called enharmonics.

Notes at this end of the neck produce a crisp, clear tone, so they are good for playing solos.

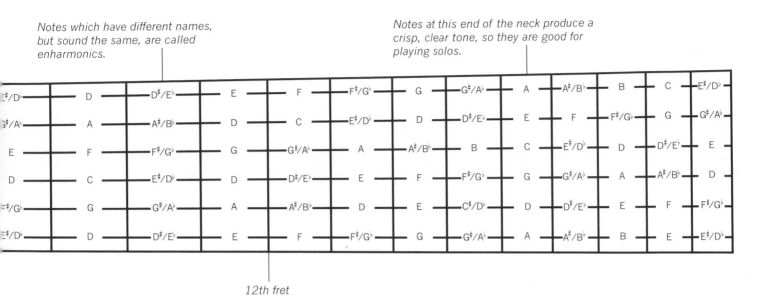

12th fret

Chord chart

Below are some of the most common chords. You can find out how to read the chord diagrams on page 15. A letter above a chord tells you which chord it is.

A small m after the letter tells you it is a minor chord (see page 34), and a 7 after the letter tells you to add the 7th note of the scale (see page 34).

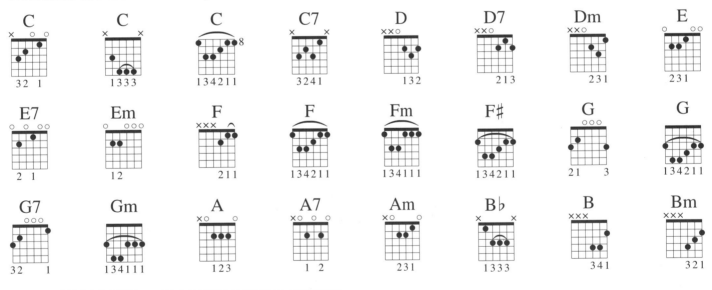

Three-chord sequences

You can make up a three-chord sequence in any key by playing the chords starting on the first, fourth and fifth notes of a scale (see page 16). This is often

known as the three-chord trick. Below, you can find out what these chords are in some of the most common keys.

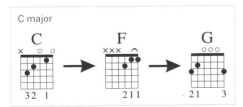

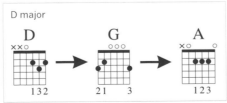

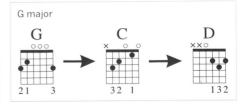

INDEX

Acknowledgements

The publishers would like to thank the following for the use of photographic material:

London Features International Ltd. (page 3, Eric Clapton; page 13, Jimi Hendrix; page 17, Frank Zappa; page 19, Gary Moore; page 21, Sting; page 22, Bon Jovi; page 25, Jimmy Page; page 27, Bonnie Raitt; page 29, Brian May; page 36, The Sex Pistols, The Kinks, The Clash, Supergrass, Blur and Oasis; page 43, Paul Weller and Kurt Cobain)
Retna (page 29, Stevie Ray Vaughn; page 30, George Benson; page 36, The Rolling Stones and Radiohead; page 41, John McLaughlin)

Redferns (page 7, Jeff Beck; page 9, Steve Vai; page 21, Tina Weymouth; page 24, Van Halen; page 25, Joe Satriani; page 34, Bob Marley; page 36, Living Colour and R.E.M.; page 38, recording studio; page 41, Poison Ivy; page 42, Prince and Pete Townsend)
Val Wilmer (page 27, Pat Metheny; page 29, Ry Cooder; page 32, B. B. King)
The models in the photographs on page 4 were Isaac Quaye (left) and Joe Pedley (right). The publishers would also like to thank Rhodes Music Co. Ltd., London, and Andy's Guitar Centre and Workshop, London, for supplying the instruments in the photos.

#7215

7215